P9-DDW-721

HOW? WHO? WHAT? WHEN? WHERE? WHY?

Questions kids ask

ABOUT
WORDS AND EXPRESSIONS

PUBLISHER	Joseph R. DeVarennes	
PUBLICATION DIRECTOR	Kenneth H. Pearson	
ADVISORS	Roger Aubin	
	Robert Furlonger	
EDITORIAL SUPERVISOR	Jocelyn Smyth	
PRODUCTION MANAGER	Ernest Homewood	
PRODUCTION ASSISTANTS	Martine Gingras	Kathy Kishimoto
	Catherine Gordon	Peter Thomlison
CONTRIBUTORS	Alison Dickie	Nancy Prasad
	Bill Ivy	Lois Rock
	Jacqueline Kendel	Merebeth Switzer
	Anne Langdon	Dave Taylor
	Sheila Macdonald	Alison Tharen
	Susan Marshall	Donna Thomson
	Pamela Martin	Pam Young
	Colin McCance	
SENIOR EDITOR	Robin Rivers	
EDITORS	Brian Cross	Ann Martin
	Anne Louise Mahoney	Mayta Tannenbaum
PUBLICATION ADMINISTRATOR	Anna Good	
ART AND DESIGN	Richard Comely	Ronald Migliore
	Robert B. Curry	Penelope Moir
	George Elliott	Marion Stuck
	Marilyn James	Bill Suddick
	Robert Johanssen	Sue Wilkinson

Canadian Cataloguing in Publication Data

Main entry under title:

Questions kids ask about words and expressions

(Questions kids ask ; 25)
ISBN 0-7172-2564-X

1. Language and languages—Miscellanea—Juvenile literature.
2. English language—Miscellanea—Juvenile literature.
3. Figures of speech—Miscellanea—Juvenile literature.
4. Children's questions and answers.
I. Smyth, Jocelyn.   II. Comely, Richard.   III. Series.

P124.Q48 1988   j400   C89-093174-7

Copyright © 1989 by Grolier Limited. All rights reserved.
Printed and Bound in U.S.A.

Questions Kids Ask . . .
about WORDS and EXPRESSIONS

continued

What language do dogs speak?

Dogs are clever animals. They can be taught to follow orders in any language. But what language do they speak? You might think a Norwegian elk hound would only speak Norwegian and a Chow would only understand Chinese. This simply isn't true. Dogs only communicate in one language—dog language. So if you have an English foxhound and a French poodle and you ask them both to speak, they will both "bow wow"—and they'll understand each other perfectly.

DID YOU KNOW . . . people who speak different languages have different ways of expressing the sounds animals make. For instance, English speakers believe a rooster says cock-a-doodle-doo, French speakers think it says cocorico and Italians interpret it as chicchirichi.

What is a rebus puzzle?

Do you like puzzles? And do you get tired of reading and writing in the same old way? Then you might like rebus writing.

Rebus uses picture words. So in this unusual language you can use pictures, numbers and letters combined in whatever way you want.

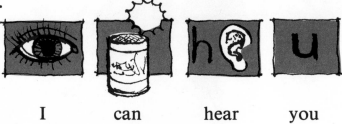

I   can   hear   you

Rebuses were originally used in semiprimitive societies to simplify difficult words or phrases.

* I will be home by sundown.

Does a word in one language always match a single word in another language?

Every language has words which can't be translated into another language without adding more words to get the idea across. A good example is the word "mamihlapinatapai" used in southern Argentina and Chile. The English translation of this word is "looking at each other hoping that either will offer to do something which both parties desire but are unwilling to do." Try to find one word in any other language which says all that!

What is a coat of arms?

Did you think a coat of arms had more arms than a regular coat? Or did you picture it as a coat made out of arms? Both are wrong. In fact, coats of arms were originally used to help people separate friends from enemies on the battle field.

In the 12th century, when knights wore armor and helmets in battle, it was difficult to tell one person from another. So knights painted their shields with various colors, patterns and figures to identify themselves. Then they could tell who was friendly and who to fight. Later these designs were also painted on tunics, or coats. These coats covered the knights' armor—and the term coat of arms evolved. Although coats of arms aren't as important today as they once were, many people are still proud of their family crest.

How many different languages are spoken in the world?

Since earliest days, people have been trying to communicate with each other. Over time, the grunts and murmurs of cave people grew into sounds which, when grouped together, formed a language. Today, there are between 3000 and 4000 different languages spoken in the world. However, only 13 of these are widely used. They are: Chinese, English, Russian, Spanish, Hindi, Italian, Arabic, Bengali, Portuguese, Japanese, German, Malay-Indonesian, and French. Each of these languages is spoken by over 50 million people.

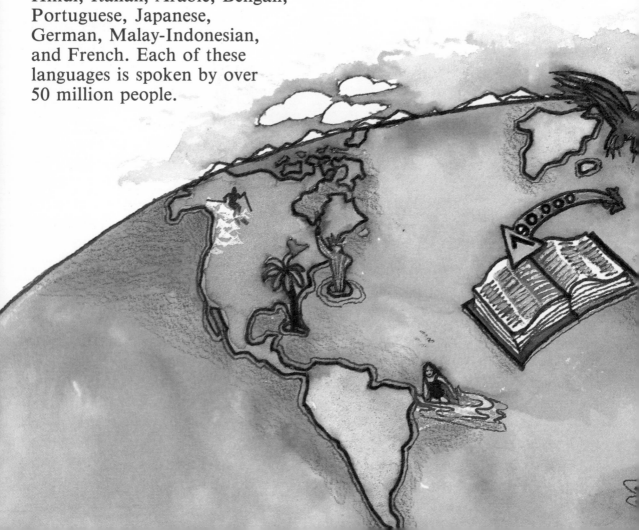

What language has the most words?

If you were to list every word in the English language it would take a long time—and a lot of paper! English has the most words of any language—790 000 of them. Try remembering how to spell that many words!

Which language is spoken by the most people?

If you thought the country with the most people must have the language spoken by the most people in the world, then you're absolutely correct.

China has the world's largest population—more than a billion people. More people in the world speak Chinese than any other language. English is the second most commonly spoken language, and Spanish ranks third.

Why is a book of maps called an atlas?

In Greek mythology, Atlas was the giant who held the earth on his shoulders. He was given this difficult task because he fought with Zeus, the king of the gods.

So how did a Greek god become part of a book? In 1595, Gerardus Mercator included a picture of Atlas supporting the earth on his shoulders opposite the title page of a collection of maps. He called it an atlas and the name quickly caught on.

DID YOU KNOW . . . the top vertebra of the backbone which supports the skull is called the atlas.

What is a proverb?

When people say "don't count your chickens before they've hatched," they are quoting a proverb.

A proverb is a short, witty saying which offers advice and is easy to remember. Proverbs have been around for a long time and are considered the wisdom of ordinary people. They are based on everyday experience and the observation of human nature and are often passed on by parents to children as reminders of how to behave.

There are proverbs for almost any occasion. Here are a few: "Too many cooks spoil the broth." "You can't judge a book by its cover." "An apple a day keeps the doctor away." and "Don't cry over spilt milk." What other proverbs do you know?

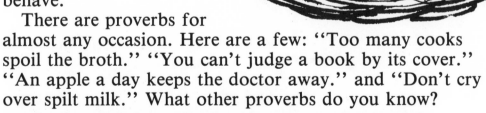

DID YOU KNOW . . . the English word with the most meanings is *set,* which has 126 meanings as a verb, 58 meanings as a noun and 10 meanings as an adjective, for a total of 194.

Where are you if you're between the devil and the deep blue sea?

You're in big trouble, that's where, because it means you're faced with two equally bad choices.

We have sailors to thank for this expression. During sea voyages sailors not only had to sail the ship, they also had to keep it in good repair. One of the most important tasks was making the ship waterproof. The toughest spot to waterproof on a wooden ship was the seam nearest the keel, just above the water line. Sailors nicknamed this seam "the devil." Waterproofing the seam was a hard job because the sailor was literally between the "devil" (the seam) and the "deep blue sea" (the ocean). If he accidentally lost his footing he could fall in the water and drown.

What is a red herring?

Believe it or not there aren't any red herrings in the sea. But you can eat a red herring. How is this possible? A special smoking process causes herrings to turn a reddish color and it also gives them a very strong smell. It is so strong that it can confuse even an expert tracking dog, making it lose the original scent it was following.

But a red herring can confuse more than dogs. It is more than just a fish—it's a term used to describe something that distracts you while you're supposed to be concentrating on something else. In a murder mystery, the author might use a red herring, or false clue, to throw readers off the murderer's trail.

What's the longest word in the world?

The next time you're at a Greek restaurant, try ordering a dish with 17 sweet and sour ingredients. You'd better not be in a hurry, because it's the longest word in the world with 182 letters. Translated, it means "a meal composed of pieces of meat dipped in honey and ouzo with cucumbers and pickles." Now that's a mouthful!

What is the longest word in the English language?

If you've seen the movie *Mary Poppins,* you'll remember the word *supercalifragilisticexpialidocious.* Is it the longest word in the English language?

It is 34 letters long but it doesn't count, because it isn't a real word—it was made up.

The biggest dictionary of the English language, the *Oxford English Dictionary,* lists *floccipaucinihilipilification* as its longest word. It's a real tongue-twister! It has 29 letters, and means "the act of estimating as worthless."

The *Oxford English Dictionary* may be the biggest, but *Webster's Third International Dictionary* has a longer word! It is *pneumonoultramicroscopicsilicovolcanoconiosis.* It is 45 letters long—by far the longest word in the language. Luckily, it is not a word we have to use every day: it is the name of a lung disease found only in miners.

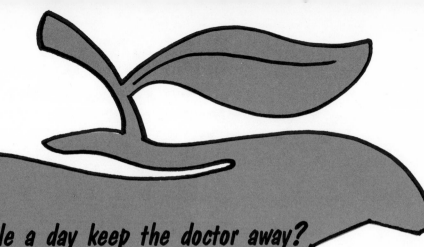

Does an apple a day keep the doctor away?

That's a popular saying, or proverb, and like a lot of folk wisdom it has a certain amount of truth to it.

Eating the proper foods is one of the best things you can do to keep yourself healthy. And apples sure are good for you. They contain vitamins C and A, and the mineral potassium. Pectin is also in apples and it helps you to digest your food. Finally, apples are full of fiber which helps with digestion. But simply eating an apple each day without doing other important things to keep yourself healthy isn't going to keep the doctor away.

DID YOU KNOW . . . people have been eating apples for 2 1/2 million years!

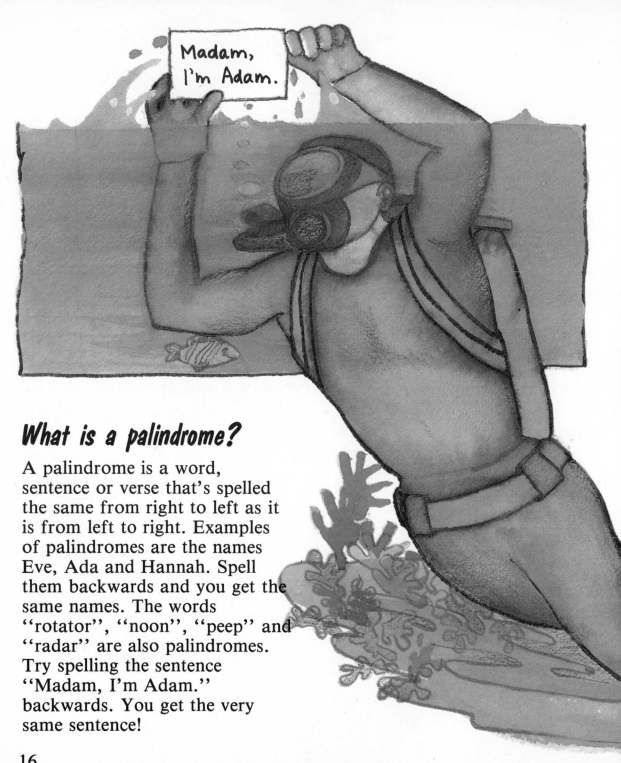

What is a palindrome?

A palindrome is a word, sentence or verse that's spelled the same from right to left as it is from left to right. Examples of palindromes are the names Eve, Ada and Hannah. Spell them backwards and you get the same names. The words "rotator", "noon", "peep" and "radar" are also palindromes. Try spelling the sentence "Madam, I'm Adam." backwards. You get the very same sentence!

16

What is an acronym?

The word radar is an acronym, made from **ra**dio, **d**etection **a**nd **r**anging. An acronym is a word formed from the first letters of other words.

Let's try some more. **L**ight **a**mplification by **s**timulated **e**mission of **r**adiation gives us the acronym laser. Have you ever wondered where the word "scuba" comes from? It's an acronym formed by the first letters of the words **s**elf-**c**ontained **u**nderwater **b**reathing **a**pparatus.

DID YOU KNOW . . . the longest palindrome is supposedly over 65 000 words.

What is an ideogram?

You are able to read this book because you have learned 26 symbols called letters which represent the sounds that make up our language. Placed in the right order, these sound symbols produce written words.

But not everyone uses an alphabet based on sound. The Chinese have a writing system composed of characters called ideograms. In many ways an ideogram is like a drawing of the thing it represents. Each ideogram represents a whole idea, not just one sound.

You've probably used or read ideograms yourself without knowing it. In arithmetic the signs " + " and "-" tell us to either add or subtract numbers.

DID YOU KNOW . . . a Chinese student must learn about 3500 different ideograms to read a simple novel.

Who was the real McCoy?

If you've got the "real McCoy," you've got the real thing, not a fake.

The expression began in the 1890s when a prizefighter named Kid McCoy traveled from town to town winning boxing matches. Kid McCoy became so well known that other boxers would claim to be him to attract a larger crowd to their match and make more money. The story goes that one day a man who had seen several of these fake McCoys lose bragged that he wasn't afraid of any McCoy. Unfortunately for him, the real prizewinning boxer was in the room. The Kid then knocked him to the floor, whereupon the man was heard to add . . . "except the real McCoy!"

Do you have holes in your head?

WHAT WAS THAT YOU ASKED THERE BUDDY?

Sometimes when you see people acting strangely you may wonder, "Are they crazy?" or "Do they have holes in their head?" What you really mean is, "Is their common sense escaping through the holes in their head?"

Are there holes in *your* head? Of course! Everyone's head has holes. Count how many you have. If you are like most of us you'll find seven—two ears, two eyes, two nostrils and one mouth.

These holes are your body's doors and windows to the outside world. It's through these holes that you find out about the world and get things from the world into your body. You hear sounds through your ears.

You see through your eyes. You smell through your nostrils and taste through your mouth. All your food and air comes through these last three holes as well.

Maybe the next time you see people acting foolishly you should ask: "Do they have *extra* holes in their head?"

DID YOU KNOW . . . the longest place name in the world is Taumatawhakatangihangakoauauotamatea (turipukakapi-kimaungahoronuku) pokaiwhenvakitanatahu. It is the unofficial name of a hill in Southern Hawke's Bay, New Zealand and it translates as "the place where Tamatea, the man with the big knee who slid, climbed and swallowed mountains, known as Land-eater, played on his flute to his loved one."

How many words are there for snow?

That depends on what language you're speaking. In English there is only one word—snow—while the Eskimo, or Inuit, language of Inuktitut has over 40 words! Each one describes a different type of snow. *Sitilluqaq* is hard snow that is used to build an Inuit home, or igloo. *Maujaq* is soft snow and *aumannaqtq* is very soft snow. Since snow is such an important part of the Inuit people's lives they have many words for it.

Likewise the Australian aborigines who speak Pintupi have many words for hole. A *yulpilpa* is a burrow for small animals and a *mutara* is a special hole in a spear. These people who hunt "down under" need a variety of words to describe different kinds of holes.

So if you can't find an English word to describe something, you may just have to borrow a word from another language.

Why do people speak different languages?

If there were only as many people in the world as there are in your classroom, there probably would only be one language spoken. That is if everyone stayed in the same place.

Wherever people are, there's sure to be language. No one knows how and when people began speaking to each other, but there are many theories.

There are between 3000 and 4000 different tongues, or languages, spoken the world over. Most of them are very different from the English language.

Languages can evolve in many ways. Some people believe all languages came from one original tongue. But as the world's population increased, some people moved away. They made up words for the new things they discovered on their travels. After a while, they began speaking in a different way from the people they had left behind.

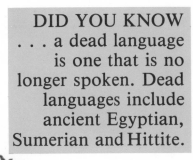

DID YOU KNOW . . . a dead language is one that is no longer spoken. Dead languages include ancient Egyptian, Sumerian and Hittite.

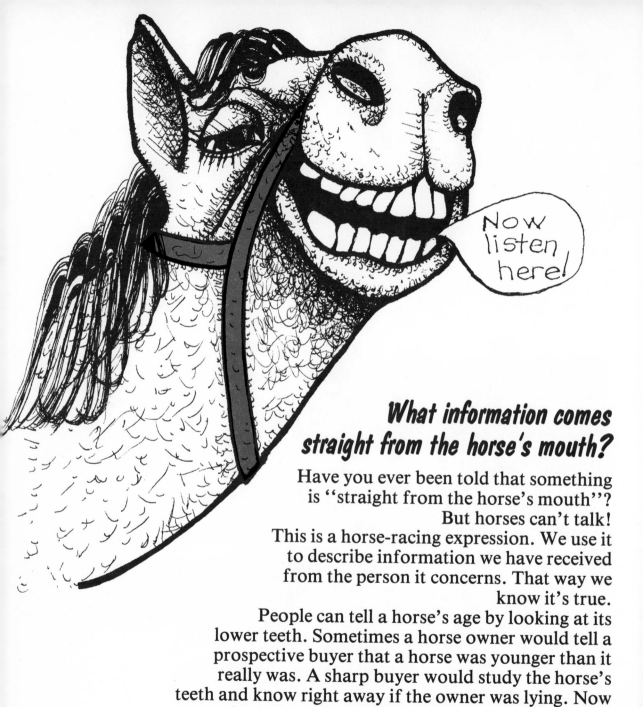

What information comes straight from the horse's mouth?

Have you ever been told that something is "straight from the horse's mouth"? But horses can't talk! This is a horse-racing expression. We use it to describe information we have received from the person it concerns. That way we know it's true.

People can tell a horse's age by looking at its lower teeth. Sometimes a horse owner would tell a prospective buyer that a horse was younger than it really was. A sharp buyer would study the horse's teeth and know right away if the owner was lying. Now that's getting your information straight from the horse's mouth!

How do you let the cat out of the bag?

If you've ever ruined someone's plans by telling a secret, then you've "let the cat out of the bag." In England long ago, farmers carried their pigs to market in a bag slung over their shoulders. Sometimes people would try to sell a cat this way, pretending it was a pig. When a customer demanded to see what was in the bag before buying it, out popped the cat—and the secret! Needless to say, the trickster's plan was ruined.

How do you get a bee in your bonnet?

Don't panic if someone tells you there's a bee in your bonnet. It doesn't mean a real bee is in your hat waiting to sting you. This is an old saying which means you have a fixed idea in your mind, or you are obsessed by something. The expression probably comes from what some people saw as the seemingly aimless buzzing of bees in the hive.

What is an Achilles' heel?

Achilles was a great hero in Greek mythology. Soon after his birth, his mother dipped him in the Styx, the river of the underworld, to make him immortal. It would have worked except that the water did not touch the heel by which she held him. Achilles was later slain during the Trojan War by an arrow wound in his one vulnerable or weak spot—his heel.

To have an Achilles' heel means to have a weakness which could lead to your downfall. Usually it is a weakness in character such as pride, jealousy, ambition or an uncontrollable temper.

What are crocodile tears?

Crocodiles don't really cry. But the ancient Egyptians living near the Nile River believed that a crocodile cried as he gobbled someone up for dinner. The crocodiles were not crying because they were unhappy; their false tears were used to lure their unfortunate victims to them.

DID YOU KNOW . . . the strong tendon at the back of the ankle that attaches the calf muscle to the heel bone is called the Achilles tendon, also after the hero Achilles.

"Crocodile tears" is an expression that developed from this story. People who cry "crocodile tears" are pretending to weep or to show sorrow they do not really feel. Like the legendary crocodiles, these people are only acting sad. Don't fall for someone's crocodile tears—they're insincere.

Who said "let them eat cake"?

If someone offered you a piece of cake, I'm sure you would say "yes." But when Marie Antoinette told the French peasants to "eat cake," she wasn't trying to be nice.

Marie Antoinette was the Queen of France from 1774 to 1793. She was the wife of King Louis XVI.

The French government was very poor when Marie Antoinette became queen. Nevertheless, she spent a great deal of money on clothes and jewelry for herself and on expensive furniture for the French palace at Versailles.

During the time she was queen, France suffered a huge crop failure and many people had nothing to eat. When Marie Antoinette was told that the peasants had no bread, it is claimed that she replied: "Then let them eat cake!" Her answer showed that she did not care about the poor conditions in France and how the people were suffering. The people grew angrier as their situation worsened and in 1789 they began a revolution.

When the revolutionaries took control of France they charged Louis and Marie Antoinette with treason. They were tried and found guilty, and both were beheaded in 1793.

So the next time someone offers you a piece of cake remember Marie Antoinette, for now you know how she lost her head over cake!

Did Nero really fiddle while Rome burned?

Perhaps you have heard the story about Nero, Emperor of Rome, who calmly played his fiddle while the city burned around him.

Nero was Emperor of Rome from A.D. 54 to 68. He is remembered for being one of the cruelest emperors ever. Not only did he order the deaths of many Christians, he had several of his own relatives killed as well!

Nero was more interested in playing music than in being emperor. He would often leave Rome and travel to Greece where he would participate in music festivals.

In A.D. 64 a great fire broke out in Rome. It burned for almost ten days. Thousands of people died and most of the city was destroyed.

Nero was accused of starting the fire to make room for a new palace he wanted to build. It is also said that he didn't even try to help save the people who were trapped in the flaming city. This led to the saying that "Nero fiddled while Rome burned."

Today if a person does not help when there is an emergency, we say that the person "fiddled while Rome burned." The saying goes back to the emperor who would rather have been a musician!

What kind of salt is the salt of the earth?

Salt is something that has many uses—we depend on it to improve the flavor of food and to preserve meat and vegetables. This useful substance is very easy to find in oceans and some lakes and also under the ground.

"Salt of the earth" is an old expression that describes people who, like salt, can be depended on. Salt found underground is part of the earth's foundations—people who are the "salt of the earth" are as stable and reliable as the earth itself.

DID YOU KNOW . . . long ago, Roman soldiers were paid not in money but in salt. The Latin word for salt, *sal,* gives us the word "salary."

What are the antipodes?

It depends where you are standing, because *antipodes* means "with the feet opposite." Imagine that you are standing near the North Pole, so that your feet are directly opposite the South Pole. You could then say that the people and places around the South Pole are the antipodes. However, the opposite is also true. A person at the South Pole could say that things at the North Pole are the antipodes.

The British first used antipodes to describe Australia and New Zealand because these lands are almost exactly opposite the British Isles.

What is an anagram?

If you like to play word games, anagrams is for you. In this game, you make new words from old ones. How? By rearranging the letters of a word or phrase to spell a new one. Be sure to use every letter. Here are some anagrams: evil (live), rose (sore), real (earl), and acre (care).

There are also some famous and difficult anagrams. Florence Nightingale forms "Flit on cheering angel." Queen Victoria's Jubilee becomes "I require love in a subject."

How much tea is there in China?

You've probably heard people say that they wouldn't give something up for "all the tea in China." It's an old saying that means that they wouldn't trade it for anything in the world.

According to an ancient Chinese legend, tea was discovered by the emperor Shen-Nung in 2737 B.C., when some leaves from a wild tea bush fell into his drinking water as it was being boiled. He enjoyed the flavor of the brewed tea leaves as he drank what legend says was the world's first cup of tea.

Today, tea is produced by many countries around the world. India is the largest tea producer, but China is a close second. It produces over 360 000 metric tons each year. So if a person ever refuses to give you up "for all the tea in China," you can consider yourself very highly valued indeed.

What's a white elephant?

If you're ever offered a white elephant, you'd be wise to refuse. "White elephant" is a term used to mean an expensive, but useless, possession.

In ancient Siam, present-day Thailand, whenever a white elephant was captured, it immediately became the property of the king. It was against the law to kill the animal. The king would probably give the white elephant to someone who had made him angry. Since the elephant was very expensive to take care of and it was against the law to destroy it, the keeper was certain to face financial ruin.

At a white elephant sale at a bazaar you will find many useless items for sale.

Index _____